©1996 Stephen Shakeshaft

Published by:
Liverpool Daily Post and Echo
PO Box 48
Old Hall Street
Liverpool

ISBN 1 872568 33 5

Book production by:
The Bluecoat Press (Liverpool)

Page make-up and typesetting by:
March Design (Liverpool)

Origination by:
Tenon and Polert Colour Scanning

NO ILLUSIONS

Behind the Headlines: Thirty years as a newspaper photographer

Stephen Shakeshaft

with words by
Angela Candlin

Foreword

In London, 1974, an unsuspecting Liverpudlian with his first play about to open in the West End, I dutifully followed my producer's instructions and turned up for my first ever meeting with press photographers.

I have never been the same since. I couldn't believe some of the things they required me to do. Stand outside a theatre in broad daylight, in full view of the public, with a script in one hand and a quill (yes a quill) in the other; pose on the Eros plinth wearing a red and white football scarf; one photographer actually brought along a Beatle wig (the play in question was about The Beatles) and wanted me to pose in wig and mime playing an air guitar. One inspired master of the lens had discovered I was then still a teacher. He wanted me to pose outside the theatre in mortar board and gown.

No doubt you see then why I now have an absolute dread of photographers. Following that early encounter I learned to try and avoid those who wanted me to pose in some particular setting or to wield some ridiculous but supposedly significant prop.

And then I met Steve Shakeshaft. I was reluctant, terribly reluctant. The press officer at the Playhouse said something about a picture with some of the kids and mentioned bubble gum. Assuming that the bubble gum was strictly for the kids, I turned up at the shoot and was promptly handed two sticks of Hubba Bubba. The guy handing me the gum had a single camera slung around his neck, and apparently quite blind to my look of horror as I realised he was expecting me to start blowing bubbles, he quickly guided me into position. Before I knew what was going on, I was blowing gum along with the kids and he was clicking away.

Wondering just how the hell I'd been charmed into doing this thing and dreading seeing the result, I wandered off muttering curses on Beatle wigs, bubble gum and beguiling press photographers.

A few hours later I saw the photograph in the paper, one of the very few which I really treasure. Since then I have come to understand that Steve Shakeshaft is a true master of the lens. For him, and him only, I have subsequently and without the merest murmur of complaint sprawled on a sun lounger at the Albert Dock in the middle of winter, secure in the knowledge that if Steve says it will come out looking something like Mediterranean Merseyside, then that's how it will be. And that's how it was.

For him, and only him, I'd hang off the girders on Runcorn Bridge, hokey cokey along Lime Street with the Tap Dancing Poets, do cartwheels in Canning Street. And even wear a Beatle wig.

Willy Russell 1996

Introduction

A press photographer is a professional observer. There is a lot of pretentious talk about the art of photography and the technical side of cameras. But the skill is to capture the moment and the camera is only the tool, in the way a plumber would regard a wrench. I can never get excited by cameras. They need to be good, expensive and to work. That's all.

The picture is taken in your head – I'm always taking pictures even when I'm not holding a camera. That black box just puts it on to film.

The adrenaline for a press photographer is intense and immediate. It comes from knowing that you may only get one chance at a picture. We're always insecure even if we think we've got a good shot. It's why we say "It makes a good picture but I haven't seen the negative yet." We only ever relax when we do see it. The subject's eyes could be closed or that vital frame missed by a five hundredth of a second.

The basics of the job will never change despite digital cameras, photographers' cars as mobile darkrooms and electronic picture desks.

The big difference between a photographer and a reporter is that the press cameraman has to be there. He can't do the job by phone or catch up later with a quote. If he misses the picture – it's gone forever.

Rushing it back for edition time is also challenging. The best picture in the world is useless even a minute after the paper goes to press.

So the three imperatives are: get there, get the picture, get back.

The discipline of working to a deadline for a daily paper can be stressful, exhausting and exhilarating. Addictive too.

Reporters tend to work in packs. Photographers are loners, concentrating one hundred per cent on the picture. If it happens in front of the lens you must be ready. You can't ask a jockey to do an action replay of a crashing fall at Becher's Brook because you weren't quick enough. Some photographers try to cover themselves by taking hundreds of shots, but I've always felt that was pointless. It means you never have complete confidence in yourself.

Press photographers may not have the luxury of time, but once you see the picture and know it's right, you take it instinctively.

Looking through life with a photographer's eye is interesting, thought provoking, poignant, sometimes upsetting and often funny. I hope the selection in this book – taken over the last thirty years for the Liverpool Daily Post and Echo – reflects it.

Anyone considering a career as a press cameraman should develop one very useful skill. The art of running backwards. It's absolutely essential when covering cup finals and royal visits. After all the readers want to see the faces and that means running backwards in front of the action. I hope to carry on running backwards into the next century.

Stephen Shakeshaft

The Pope was arriving at Liverpool Airport by helicopter. The visit was planned in fine detail, hundreds of well wishers waited and so did the photographers. Yards of telephoto lens were trained on the Pope as he appeared in the doorway. A sudden gust of wind snatched his skull cap and blew it towards the Mersey. Our camera shutters sounded like exploding firecrackers.

Only in Liverpool could you have an ex-policeman as a Pope lookalike. The faces in the bus queue look unimpressed. Unlike the sign on the lorry in the background, Mr Bird was far from original.

First Royal tour after the honeymoon. Look at the body language. They both seem so unsure. This was before Diana became a fashion icon and learned that the camera loved her. On the first Royal tour after the honeymoon, Charles and Diana went to Caernarfon. She was stick thin, the clothes looked frumpy, as if she was wearing someone else's, and that hat, so awkward. The crowd adored shy Di and we focused on that reaction. Eventually Prince Charles' bodyguard strode across and asked us to take a few pictures of Charles because Diana was getting all the attention.

Prince Charles often asks cameramen how far we've travelled and have we taken any good pictures. As he approached us on one royal visit, he put his hand in his pocket, pulled out a library ticket and looked astonished. His entourage came to a sudden stop behind him as if brakes had been applied. "I seem to have a library ticket in my jacket. I haven't been in for a library book, have I?" he asked his equerry. The London photographer next to me chipped in. "Hope there isn't a fine to pay, sir." "Yes, quite," replied a bemused Charles.

Often Royal watchers who've waited hours in all weathers are struck dumb when an HRH actually stops to talk. One woman, clutching her scrapbook of pictures of Prince Charles, was so excited she couldn't contain herself. "Charles, dear , over here." But when he came and smiled at her she was speechless. Then she burst out "Eeh, you look just like your photo."

News editors have a wicked sense of humour. "Charles is walking up Snowdon today," he said. "You walk with him." Dressed for climbing in waterproofs and a woolly hat, I was amazed that the Prince of Wales was in slacks, a sports jacket, collar and tie. "Good morning, gentlemen, hope you are fit," he said, striding past. He was younger, fitter and not burdened by a heavy camera bag round his neck. We jumped streams, scrambled over walls, climbed many stiles and panted along, trying to keep up with him. In a forest on a hill outside Dolgellau we stopped for lunch. It was bizarre. Sitting on a mountainside having a picnic with the Prince of Wales. An aide came across. "His Royal Highness would prefer it if you did not take a picture of him eating hard boiled eggs." Fair enough. God knows why.

The most relaxed of the fifty plus Royal visits I've covered was when Princess Diana went to Ford's Halewood factory. No stiffness or stuffiness. This relaxed shot of her with the girls in the car upholstery section won Kodak's Royal Picture of the Year award in 1988.

As a trainee I was the only photographer on a fixed point outside the Empire Theatre for a royal gala. Anxiously I kept double checking my camera to make sure it worked, to a duty policeman's amusement. The Queen's limo drew up, she emerged and I held up the camera to my eye. She stumbled slightly, so I hesitated before pressing the shutter. Then I set the flash off, the Queen smiled straight into the lens and I had a good picture.
  A few days later, I received a message from the Lord Lieutenant's office . The Queen had commented on the photographer waiting until she composed herself before taking the picture. It wouldn't have happened in London, she said.

Out campaigning on a windy Crosby promenade, SDP candidate Shirley Williams was looking out to sea when a gust of wind caught her skirt and she was frozen in classic Marilyn Monroe pose.

An immaculate Michael Heseltine was touring the city black spots with a coach of potential investors he was hoping to impress. Despite his good intentions he was pelted with eggs by protesters. I found out later – and this sums up Liverpool humour – that one of the culprits left a note for her husband. "I'm out protesting. Your dinner's on Mr Heseltine."

Frank's greasy spoon cafe on the Dock Road wins
accolades in good food guides. I took Jeffrey Archer
there for a bacon buttie. His palate was jaded after
months on the rubber chicken circuit, drumming up
support for the Tories. He sat there among the
dockers in his Savile Row suit, grease dripping down
his chin. "Make yourself at home, Jeffrey. Tuck in.
Have another one," urged Frank. He did too, while
his driver paced outside, staring at his watch. "Wait
till I get back to Westminster and tell them about your
bacon butters," he drooled. "Butties, Jeffrey, butties,"
corrected Frank. Now he makes detours whenever
he's on Merseyside and has been promoted to the
seat of honour, a high stool in the kitchen next to
Frank's deep fat fryer.

Passive smoking is an occupational hazard for photographers. The worst place was at the front of Harold Wilson's press conferences, coughing and choking from that dreaded pipe. I always suspected it was a ploy, giving him time to think as he fiddled to get it re-lit. This time I dodged the flame from his killer lighter and escaped with singed eyebrows.

They sang "For he's a jolly good fellow" to Ted Heath after his speech at a Liverpool hotel. He loved it. He didn't love it quite so much when I asked to take his picture on another occasion, drinking a pint in a village pub. "Mr Heath will be photographed with half a bitter," said his agent. And as he tucked into his bar meal the former Prime Minister asked in all seriousness: "Will your readers know what a ploughman's lunch is?"

Was this a tear Derek Hatton was shedding? Not likely. The rebellious deputy leader of the city council was chairing a press conference, using his unique blend of rhetoric, emotion and body language. His aftershave arrived thirty seconds ahead of him and wham – he was in your personal space faster than a departing Tory down the M62.

After the Toxteth Riots
Margaret Thatcher
arrived in Liverpool
unannounced to see
the ravages for herself.
At a press conference
later the look in those
Prime Ministerial eyes
said more than a
thousand words.

Paul McCartney brought his new band, Wings, to Liverpool. I went to the theatre and was blocked by the doorman. "Sorry," he said. "Paul has his own security staff and no one gets in." Undeterred, I slipped in the back because I've learned it's not the stars who don't want to be photographed or talk to the Press, but the bureaucrats around them. "Come on in," said Paul. It was like stepping into someone's private world. The McCartneys were in their Sunday scruff. Linda was there without tights on and the kids were running up and down the corridor playing tag. Paul is one of the most straight-forward people I have ever photographed. No superstar silliness and no professional Scouser clichés either. Dusty Springfield demanded to choose the angle of my photograph, Richard Carpenter wouldn't put his arm around sister Karen and a seventies sex kitten stripped naked in front of me. They were all strong personalities – once I got past the red tape.

It all ended in tears when The Beatles took a British Rail ticket to ride to Bangor, north Wales for a weekend of spiritual contemplation with their guru, the Maharishi Yogi. With them went Mick Jagger, Marianne Faithfull, the world's press and me. I was photographing Paul McCartney in the university quadrangle when the phone shrilled in the porter's lodge. Paul answered it and went white. "Brian's dead. I must tell the boys," he said, aghast. The death of their manager and mentor, Brian Epstein was the end of those innocent flower power days. A black limo took them back to London in the rain.

Comedian Les Dawson had a scowl like an angry bulldog as he sat in the dressing room in Y-fronts, hairy, perspiring heavily, with a gin and tonic in hand. It was a stifling July night. The last thing he wanted was to get into an evening suit and go on stage. He put his eye to the curtain and reported back. "There won't be many laughs tonight. It's as hot as hell out there and they all look knackered."

Doddy goes back to his old school in Knotty Ash.
In my early days, I was backstage at the Royal Court
Theatre at 5.15 pm for Doddy's first show at six. Ten
minutes before the curtain went up there was no sign of
him. Taciturn Norman, the stage doorman who'd seen it all
before, poured me another mug of tea. "Give him five
minutes yet." Suddenly the wind blew Doddy, hanging on
to his trilby, into the tiny hallway. "By jove, Norman, what
a night. Keep the cat in." "Now young man, what can I do
for you?" he asked. As I told him he said "come into the
dressing room. Help yourself to a lager." He stripped down
to his woolly vest, applied a quick dab of make-up, took off
his hat and rumpled his hair with his fingers as if his head
had been in a spin dryer. As the orchestra was half way
through his intro music he grabbed his moggy coat – a
long, tomato red fur with big yellow buttons. "Back in ten
minutes, have another lager."
I sat alone in the dressing room listening to the opening
salvo of jokes on the speaker. All around me were Doddy's
props, tickling sticks, drums, Dicky Mint his vent's dummy,
jackets every colour of the rainbow and a life size rubber
cow. Pieces of paper were spread all over the place, each
with a storyline or punch line to a joke.

"I don't care who you are, you won't be allowed
to take a photograph of Dame Margot." The press
assistant was in a difficult mood. Luckily I was on
good terms with the stage door attendant at the
Royal Court Theatre. A dressing room door
opened, Dame Margot wanted a cup of tea. I
introduced myself. "Come in," she invited, "please
take whatever pictures you want." For half an
hour she sat talking, brave enough to be
photographed, as few women would, in a
dressing gown with an unmade face.
Transformation complete, she asked me to stand
in the wings with my camera. A few weeks later,
in the same dressing room, the star of a sex revue
asked "what kind of photo do you want?" and
promptly dropped her dressing gown and stood
there naked.

22

Standing in the wings of a theatre I am intrigued the way the curtain separates fantasy from reality. In the moments before it rose for a performance of Swan Lake at the Liverpool Empire I was a silent witness to a secret ritual. Like butterflies caught in a net, the members of the Royal Ballet fluttered and dipped, stretched and preened. Straps were adjusted, hair titivated, one ballerina still in her towelling dressing gown. Young girls, fragile as fairies, yet fitter than footballers.

Forget the pyjama striped suit, the spats, the trademark hat, the exuberant tie. With this glacial stare the normally rumbustious jazz singer George Melly could be former Prime Minister Ted Heath's double. Something to do with the jawline, perhaps.

Peter Cushing. Man of Horror – but at Albert Dock he was the perfect gentleman, rather frail dressed in a country anorak.

The shy young man with yellow hair, comedian's
specs and a conservative suit is artist David
Hockney. He's clutching a big cheque for his
winning picture, in the John Moores Exhibition, of
a naked man in a swimming pool.

A day at the beach in Southport used to be Frankie Vaughan's only boyhood holiday. A lifetime on from his backstreet upbringing in Liverpool the crooner took his wife, Stella, for a nostalgic walk through the sandhills. This time he went by Rolls Royce and chauffeured me back to the theatre after I'd taken this updated holiday snap.

A hang dog expression and a very weird choice of headgear for Seve Ballesteros during a warm up round at Royal Birkdale. Golfers can be very touchy. A past open champion blamed the sound of my shutter for his missed shot. He was just playing badly. I pointed out that I only pressed it after his putter hit the ball. And anyway a train was passing within yards of him. How come that didn't distract him? Once in a practice round before the open an American, Doug Sanders, hit a tee shot which bounced through the green and landed next to me in a skylark's nest with three eggs. We both watched the birdie!

They don't loo
they're having
Awfully Big Ad
author Beryl Ba
and her actres
slouch in the d
the Liverpool P
rehearsal room

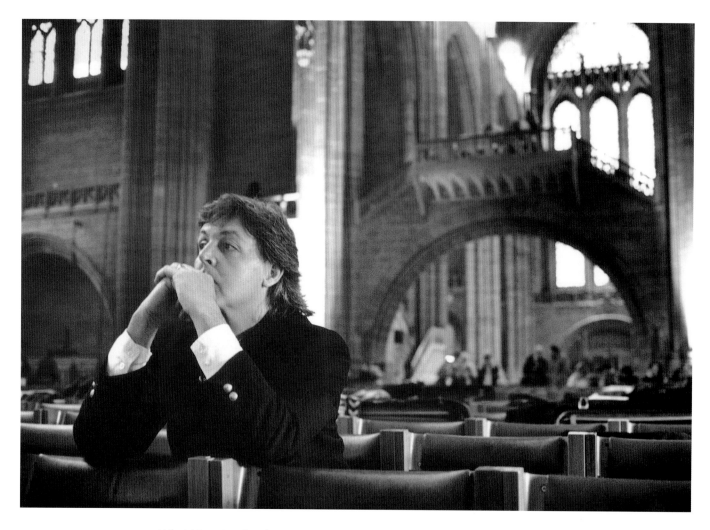

Who'd imagine that this former choirboy would be back in Liverpool Cathedral one day listening to a rehearsal by the Liverpool Philharmonic Orchestra of his oratorio. A contemplative Paul McCartney is now more establishment figure than ageing pop star.

Even living legends like Marlene Dietrich have humdrum chores like sound checks before wooing an audience. At the Liverpool Empire I focused on that amazing face, those funny boots as she went without fuss through the nuts and bolts of rehearsal. "Don't get in her line of sight and keep quiet," her personal assistant warned.

Press photographers had to be there two hours in advance when Jacko came to Aintree in 1988 for his sell-out show. Our cameras were removed in case we took pictures before it started. Then we had just three numbers to capture the definitive shot of the biggest star in world music. Ushered on stage, I was told to stand in front of the 20 ft high speakers, effectively between Jacko and his almost hysterical fans. Suddenly the sound hit me like a bomb exploding in my chest. In the crowd, a girl's body floated towards me and waiting medics on a sea of hands. The sweltering heat, the crush and the occasion were all too much. One of Jackson's heavies put a hand on my collar. Three numbers were up. We were out. Back at the office I handed in the pictures and let them make up their minds. I was stone deaf for two days.

Farewell to two Liverpool legends.
You never knew where you were with Bill
Shankly. One day I'd go to Melwood and
he'd say: "Tell me how you think the team's
playing, son." Next day I'd be there and
he'd say: "What the hell do you want?" He
always called me Peter or Big Fella, never
Steve.
He once blasted me in the team's hotel. A fire
alarm went off, Bill raced out of his room,
saw me and shouted: "What the hell are you
doing?
You've set off the alarm and you'll wake the
team." It wasn't me and I couldn't keep a
straight face – Shanks, the epitome of
Liverpool, was wearing blue pyjamas.
I took this picture the day he left. There hadn't
been as much as a whisper. In fact, that
morning he'd signed Ray Kennedy from
Arsenal. We were summoned to Anfield and
Shankly told us he was quitting. No one
knew if he meant it. He walked out and some
fans who'd been told asked him if it was true.
"Are you sorry I'm going lads?" he asked
repeatedly. Shankly – all confidence,
yet so insecure.

In a haunting echo of Bill's departure, Kenny
Dalglish walked out years later. Despite
rumours, there was the same
incomprehension.

Only Paisley could have pulled it off. He sold Kevin Keegan and atoned by signing Kenny Dalglish. The scene is the Holiday Inn in Liverpool. Keegan was back in town with Hamburg, his first return visit since leaving Anfield. I walked into the foyer as he sat reading, and before I could speak in came Dalglish and his three-year-old daughter. The two legends, arguably the greatest players in Liverpool's history, tried to chat. It was a conversation any football lover would have given a right arm to overhear. But not Kenny's daughter. She just wanted to go to bed, and left her father in no doubt where his duty lay.

The cell sized Boot Room at Anfield where famous victories were plotted over mugs of tea.

Many times a flicked cigarette stub would land on my back prompting a yell: "Hey mister, you're on fire." A bobby put the flame out once by stamping on me with his size 12 boots. One Liverpool player, out of frustration and because he wasn't particularly good, kicked my camera case when he couldn't quite reach the ball before it went out of play. I asked him if he had a cat at home. West Brom's goalie used to chat to the photographers all through the match. Another asked if I had a fag and a gin and tonic in my case. A third, a keen photographer himself, picked up my camera and kept his finger on the motor drive until the film ran out. "Fast shutter that, isn't it?" An over zealous centre forward screamed at me for not stopping the ball. He obviously hadn't read the rules of play. At a tense cup tie, the crowd pushed forward, spilling on to the pitch and the prone photographers. Police started to move some fans to another part of the stadium. With typical cheeky scouse thinking, one fan dived beside me on the groundsheet. "Give us a camera to hold, mate, and keep mum." He stayed there for the second half, giving a running commentary. Every time Liverpool came into the penalty area he shouted and waved his arms in front of my lens. Was I glad when that match was over. "Cheers, mate. Great view, do you pay to lie here?"

Crouched next to those challenging Grand National fences at Aintree, a photographer sees the unglamorous, downside – literally – of the sport of kings. There's an eerie silence, the ground vibrates to drumming hooves and we're inches away from sweating, airborne horseflesh. Jockeys swear as they're unseated, the tannoy booms, we breathe in as riderless horses swerve past outside the rails, and then silence again. I have seen many horses killed at Aintree, and I'm not proud to say that I am used to it. Sixth sense made me wait at a fence once. All the horses jumped clear and I was about to pack up and go. But a straggler, on the point of trotting back to the stables, decided to tackle the spruce. This spectacular somersault did the horse no harm, but the jockey was cursing and beating the turf in frustration as he waited for an ambulance.

I think The Chair is a more awe inspiring fence than the legendary Becher's Brook. This horse didn't survive the take off, landing in the ditch and breaking a leg. In tears, the jockey turned away and wept as he waited for the vet. I felt intrusive, wished I was invisible, as I took a few, quick pictures.

It was Grand National wonder horse Red Rum's birthday. He had more cards than the Queen Mother and tube after tube of his favourite Polo mints. His trainer, Ginger McCain, took me to the stable behind his car salesroom in the backstreets of Southport. "Rummy, someone's come to take your photograph – official birthday portrait." The three times winner of the National thrust his head over the door and gave a mighty horse laugh. So did Ginger. Ginger drove me in his truck alongside Rummy as he raced in training down the beach at Ainsdale. He hacked there, over the railway crossing, past the shops, with local children skipping by his side and calling his name. Now he's buried near the winning post at Aintree. People can scatter their relatives ashes there now.

It was before dawn as I sped up the M6. Listening to the radio broadcasts I started to realise the extent of the disaster. When I reached Lockerbie and was past the police cordons it all became unreal. There was a crater, wide and long. "That was a street," a man told me. "What do you mean?" I asked. "There was a street there," he said again. And I understood. Someone told me the plane's fuselage was on a hillside just outside the town. I found it beyond a little churchyard. There were bodies. Bodies everywhere. Rescue workers, like the man weeping in my picture, simply could not come to terms with the horror of it all. One woman found someone she thought was alive. She was wrong though. No-one could have survived. Back in the town, stunned residents were nailing slates to roofs and generally busying themselves. A Christmas tree stood in the square. I remember the creaking latch of the church gate as people made their way back and forth to that appalling, open graveyard. The wind bit cold and deep as I waited for Mrs Thatcher to arrive. The faces told it all as she left the scene of devastation. I never really understood until I started to drive home. All those people were on their way home too, to America when Pan Am Flight 103 exploded. A bomb blasted them into the sky and they lay scattered on a hillside. Contents of suitcases, so carefully packed, were strewn on the grass and the pages of passports flapped in the wind. It was the only car journey I can remember when I didn't play the radio.

Every weekend Mrs
McCourt takes a spade
and goes digging for the
body of her beloved
daughter, Helen. A man is
in prison for the murder,
but her burial place is a
mystery.

No tip-off or anything. I was up on Saddleworth Moor to do a background picture feature on that grim heath where a child's body had been discovered. Other people were there, strolling, walking dogs. Two policemen set up a tarpaulin around a piece of land 500 yards away from me. Suddenly it seemed as though every policeman in north west England had arrived. Everywhere there were officers in overalls digging with shovels. Then they brought up a tarpaulin sheet. The smell was shocking. So bad that I almost couldn't take the picture. They had found the body of another child. Soon after I was outside a magistrates' court taking a picture of Ian Brady. The Moors Murders, the Isle of Man Summerland fire disaster and the Lockerbie crash affected me more than any jobs I can remember. But many have left a stain that I can never quite scrub off. One minute you're in the office having a cup of tea and the next you're at a fatal fire or beside a motorway taking pictures of mangled bodies. Nothing prepares you, and nothing helps much afterwards. I always smile when I hear about people being counselled. No-one counsels journalists. We just get back, print our pictures, write our stories and get on with the next job. We have to counsel ourselves.

Not a film set for a disaster movie, but a clean up operation at Otterspool after a tanker leaked oil into the Mersey. The man in the wax jacket is a government minister who came to see for himself.

Granby Street school often had ten nationalities in one class. Miss Lopez, the headmistress, used to ring me on costume days.

An old man and his
grandson in the
evening light in
Liverpool's Chinatown,
the oldest Chinese
community in Europe.

A National Front rally in a New Brighton hall. The speaker was a milkman.

This picture will always haunt me. At the outbreak of the Falklands War, Captain North was detailed to skipper the massive supply ship Atlantic Conveyor. The vessel was moored at Seaforth Docks. Captain North, a likeable, gentle, Father Christmas of a man took me to his cabin. He talked about the navy, his mission and life in general. The ship was magnificent. It felt like a cathedral. I wished him luck and said that if I was going to the Falklands I'd want to be on this ship. Soon afterwards the Argentineans attacked Atlantic Conveyor, believing it was the aircraft carrier Ark Royal. The ship was sunk and Captain North went down with it.

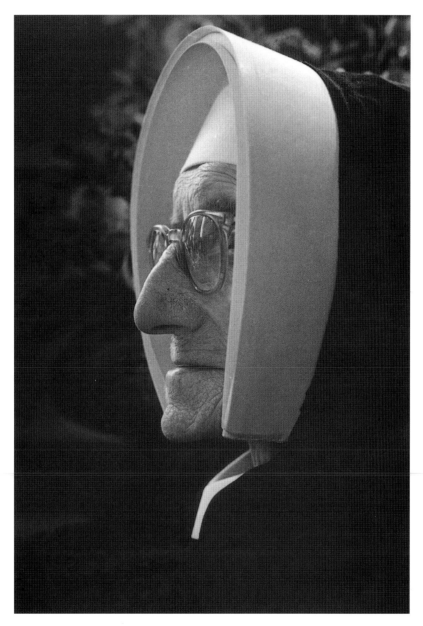

In the eyes of judges, photographers aren't journalists. We're appendages, monkeys, snappers. This picture changed their perception and won me journalist of the year. I went to a convent and took one picture that mattered of a nun in her 90s. It was her birthday. I was struck by her strong, dignified face in that great horseshoe of a headdress. A photographer is a journalist, the same as a writer. But we use a camera instead of a pen to tell a story.

Belvedere School girls walk decorously to school.

Tears of a clown. Ken Dodd was at an appeal for Claire House children's hospice. He knelt down by this little girl. His hands unconsciously mirrored hers. They both wore similar chunky boots. A beam of sunlight lit up their faces for a split second.

I first photographed Ken Dodd as a nervous, 19-year-old who didn't know quite how to approach him. He was squashed into the driving seat of a tiny Fiat car, wearing a Gannex coat and trilby. "Shakeshaft, now that's an unusual name." It must have gone into his comedy memory bank, or been written on the back of his hand. Doddy's hands always intrigue me – odd words written on his palm or shirt cuff, secret code words to remind him of a joke. Anyway I was sitting six rows from the stage at the Royal Court Theatre when he spotted me during his Christmas show. The next joke was about a jelly baby moulder called Gladys Shakeshaft. He'd remembered the name and I became part of his act ever since.

Margi Clarke rehearsing as a Scouse wicked queen in Snow White at the Empire. When she was starring as a female boxer in Blonde Fist, Margi asked me to stay behind after the photo call and be filmed letting off a flash at the ringside. But it took so long to set up the shot that I had to return to the office. My moment of stardom passed me by.

"Pose by a rose?" I asked Frank Bruno at Southport Flower Show. He chose to put a carnation, named after him, in his teeth instead. "Don't make me look stupid," he growled. I wasn't about to upset a heavyweight champ.

It looks as though I've trodden on his toe. But Carl Davis is actually shouting "Ghostbusters!" as he conducts the Royal Liverpool Philharmonic Orchestra's Summer Pops in the big top at King's Dock.

Once as famous as the Beatles, but still living a ferry ride from Merseyside, Gerry Marsden tutors an actor in the art of playing himself as a young man for the Playhouse musical, Ferry Cross the Mersey.

Flower power in the fields
of West Lancashire when a
traditional farming family
planted asters instead of
cabbages and spuds.

Catching the sun
before it sets over the
harvest.

Their two cathedrals separated by a street called Hope, the two clergymen lean on sticks chatting like the old friends they were. It was to be the last autumn for Archbishop Derek Worlock, who was recovering from surgery. He was frail and feeling the cold so I had just three minutes to take this picture in Bishop David Sheppard's garden. In Liverpool, the affectionate nickname for the dual ambassadors for the church was fish and chips – because they were always together in newspapers.

All the lonely people
... down on his luck in
a one room Liverpool
flat, John Lennon's
uncle Charlie lives
alone with his cat. He
sleeps in a Lennon
t-shirt with pictures of
the Beatles on the
nicotine stained walls.

The green grass of Anfield was a sandpit, the hallowed turf dug up for the pitch to be re-seeded. Tractors and dumper trucks manoeuvred where the gods performed Saturday afternoon miracles. I've covered matches in all weathers, flat out on a sodden groundsheet, trampled on by players long forgotten. There are stud marks on my back and a scar on my top lip where a football knocked the camera into my face as I focused. A ninety minutes soaking at Anfield in winter left me drenched, despite unfashionably heavy waterproof coat, sweaters, vests, long johns, insulated socks, fingerless gloves, scarf and woolly hat. The crowd at the Kop end loved us! They'd been waiting, shoulder to shoulder for a good hour, their faces just showing over the boundary wall. "Get your 'ead down. We've paid to come in here." Liverpool signed wingers without brakes. They kept on running until they either jumped over us or landed on top. During a European cup tie, the Bruges centre half decided to go for an impossible ball on the touchline. He landed on my back, grunting at me for being in the way. I spent the rest of the match being treated by the St. John Ambulance Brigade. In Italy, the crowd threw bottles and police dogs snapped at my ankles as Liverpool went into extra time penalties. It was normal to be on the receiving end of hurled meat pies, darts, hand gun pellets and coins – often enough to buy a round of drinks after the game.

The Morning After the Hillsborough Disaster. Sunday. Shankly Gates, Anfield. A car stopped. "Put these flowers on the gates for me, mate. I can't bear to get out." Slowly grief stricken fans were arriving at the Shankly Gates, Anfield with flowers, scarves, cards. Children, parents, grandparents. Some crying, others just standing dazed, staring at the gates. The crowd was growing. An instruction came to open the gates. In single file they walked into Anfield, straight to the Kop. They tied their colours to the goal posts, threaded flowers into the goal net. Silence. Thousands of people, yet silence. Then a Salvation Army band which had followed and formed a circle in the centre of the pitch played Abide With Me, and everyone cried. Within a few days a carpet of flowers covered the pitch. Anfield became a shrine.

Olympic cyclist Chris
Boardman unwinds
after a training session
at Hoylake.

Not all cows are mad.
Some go to the seaside for
their holidays. I was on
mine with the family on
Aberdovey beach in mid
Wales. We were
sunbathing, dozing, when
a herd of Welsh Blacks
ambled over the sandhills
and lay down next to us.
My daughter, Lucy, was
persuaded to be
photographed with them.
We all stayed till the tide
came in. It was surreal.

A customer in a leopard skin coat turns this scene outside a Seel Street emporium into an unofficial antiques roadshow.

No cat flaps for these female felines. In a dressing room at the Empire, Liverpool, it was out of jeans and t-shirts and into skin tight catsuits for the chorus girls of Cats. With whiskers and tails in place there was time to relax by re-reading letters from mum.

A Lowry-like street
scene in the snow
taken from the stand of
Everton Football Club.

Artist Frank Green
keeps a lasting
impression of old
Liverpool on canvas by
moving in with his
easel ahead of the
bulldozers with their
ball and chain.

No leisure centre for
these inner city kids.
On hot days they
jumped in the fountain
outside the Walker Art
Gallery.

Lizzie Christian was a barrow girl in Great Charlotte Street before Britain was forced to deal with EC subsidies, insecticides and standard shape bananas. She wouldn't know what a kilo was if it leapt up and bit her. Local artists used to paint her. You never see a face like that now. "How are yer, luv? Where are yer going?" she asked when I passed her stall near Lime Street Station. She always gave me an apple.

Street Life.
Harry was an opera singer with the D'Oyly Carte before life turned sour for him. Down on his luck, in baggy, second-hand trousers and filthy pumps he turned the pavement between the Playhouse and George Henry Lees department store into a stage. "The acoustics are good here," he said. That magical voice entertained an audience of shoppers and pigeons.

What the best dressed tramps are wearing. These two walked arm in arm round town. He always in a tie, she a moth eaten shawl. They posed on a bench in Williamson Square. "Official portrait is it, lad?"

Rag and bone man in
Dingle

The landlady of this dockland pub wore a different hat every day.

One man and his
horse, keeping
Birkenhead Park tidy.

House proud Scotland Road resident, aged 88, takes a breather after scrubbing her step. "Shall I put my teeth in for you?"

If we have a soul, photographers must live with guilt. We tell, in the click of a shutter, a life story of angst and despair. Then we walk away. This old lady lived by candlelight, eating from a bowl. She couldn't afford coal and the damp was thick and evil. I remember the chill to this day.
"What happened to her?" someone asked me. The answer is I don't know, except that the house was demolished. I just clicked the shutter and moved on to the next job. I saw lots of condemned properties like this. Lots of old ladies, survivors in an era of decay, with little hope but always ready to make you a cup of tea.

Bath night in the kitchen sink for the Grace children of Edge Hill in 1980. There were still up to 12,000 families in the city without a bathroom or indoor toilet.

Lady of the gaslight,
drying clothes as my
grandmother did.

An Old Contemptible, who came by bus, shoes carefully polished to pay his respects at the cenotaph on Remembrance Day.

Holly on the television is the only clue that this is Christmas day in an old folk's hostel at the Pier Head.

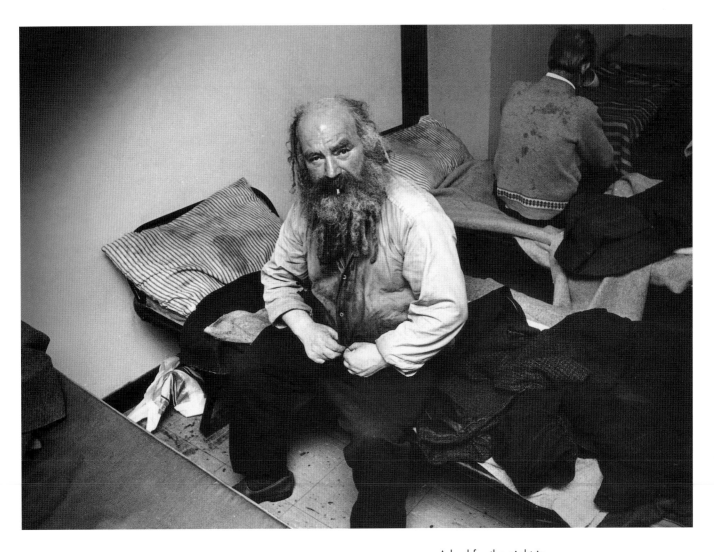

A bed for the night in
the Cathedral crypt for
a tramp. His beard is
almost an art form.

The beat goes on at this
Teddy Boys' picnic on
New Brighton promenade.

Mathew Street. I was there in the 60s when fans queued outside the Cavern. A decade later, a different sound, and punks sat on the pavement opposite at lunchtime waiting for Eric's Club to open.

The League of Welldoers
old folk's Christmas party.
One old lady nudged me.
"Don't just stand there, cut
my meat up for me."

Two housewives from Burnley earning extra cash stripping in a Liverpool pub at lunchtime. They squeezed into a broom cupboard to prepare for their act. A battered suitcase held a selection of raunchy gear, a few records to strip to, a packed lunch and a flask. Their main preoccupation was what to get the kids for tea.

Sometimes a face
jumps out of the crowd
as this did at a demo
in Toxteth.

He was 102 and lived with
his wife in one room in
Toxteth, being driven mad
by vandals.

Liverpool Anglican Cathedral, a neo-Gothic masterpiece, one of the great buildings of the world.

Fifty years a master stone mason at the Anglican Cathedral, Tom Murphy was at 80 still hoping to complete the final two angels. Agile as a trapeze artist, he worked 400 feet above the ground, climbing down for a cheese butty and a banana at midday. He'd just flown to New York to consider a contract carving in the Cathedral of St. John the Divine. "I'd be 95 when it expires," he chuckled.

Improvised cup final on
wasteland in Kirkdale.

This old lady was so proud of the flowers she grew on her allotment.

"Back garden" of a
Liverpool tenement.

High tide – dodging
the Mersey waves on
Wallasey promenade.

Out searching for a weather picture for page one of the Echo, I saw this at a bus stop. I was in a traffic jam. Pulling onto the pavement I ran across the road in the snow. It had to be spontaneous. If they'd seen me it would have ruined the effect.

On Llandudno pier for a holiday feature I saw two girls sitting in the sun on a wall. I took their picture using a wide angle lens – they thought I was photographing the view over their shoulders. If you don't make eye contact using this lens, people don't realise they are the focal point. I went for a walk and in exactly the same spot on my return were two old ladies. Click – time had moved on fifty years in ten minutes.

Pussy galore!
A majestic two and a half stone, Queenie was the fattest cat in Britain. Her daily diet included turkey breast, salmon and bran flakes. Pensioner Connie Lowndes from Rainford made her a collar of pearls and sang God Save the Queen to the once half starved alley cat she'd rescued.

Sculpture has a high
profile at the Walker
Art Gallery.